THE RAMAYAN OF TULSIDAS

THE DIVINE JOURNEY OF DHARMA AND AN OVERVIEW OF THE RAM CHARIT MANAS

DR. JAGADEESH PILLAI

Made with ♥ on the Notion Press Platform
www.notionpress.com

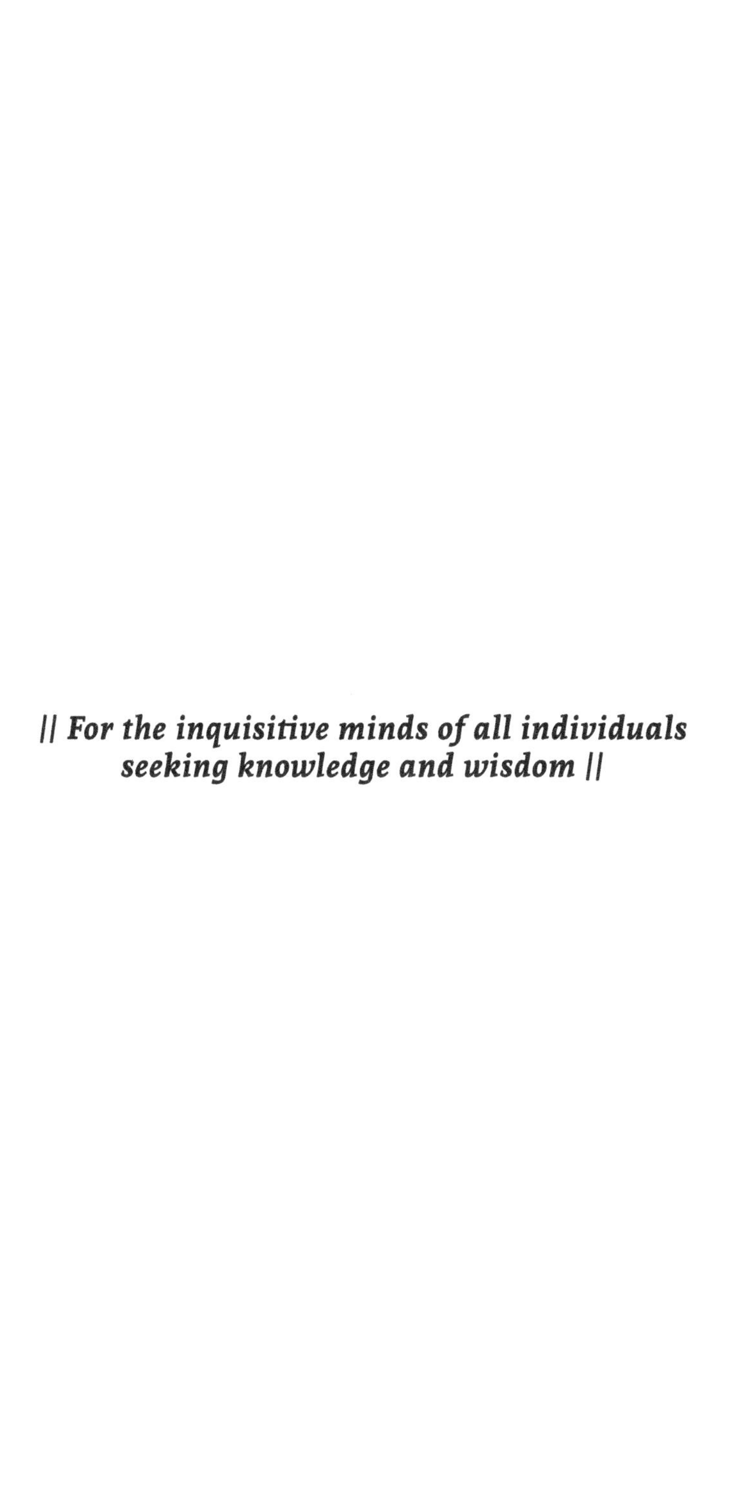

|| For the inquisitive minds of all individuals seeking knowledge and wisdom ||

Contents

Contents

Prayer

Om Shree Ganeshaya Namaha

Shri Janaki Vallabho Vijayate

Shri Ramcharitmanas

About The Author

Dr. Jagadeesh Pillai is a renowned Guinness World Record holder, writer, and researcher hailing from Varanasi, also known as the abode of Lord Shiva. With a Ph.D. in Vedic Science and a range of creative ideas and achievements, he is a true polymath. He is the author of more than 100 books including Research Publications. Although his roots can be traced back to Kerala, the people of Varanasi hold him in high regard and affectionately consider him one of their own.

Dr. Pillai has achieved four Guinness World Records in the following subjects:

"Script to Screen" - In this record, Dr. Pillai produced and directed an animation film within the shortest time possible, breaking the previous record set by Canadians. He has also received numerous national and international awards and recognitions for this achievement.

Longest Line of Postcards - For this record, Dr. Pillai created a line of 16,300 postcards on the occasion of the 163rd anniversary of Indian Postal Day. The event also included a questionnaire about the Indian flag.

Largest Poster Awareness Campaign - Dr. Pillai designed an awareness campaign on the subject of "Beti Bachao - Beti Padhao" (Save the Girl Child - Educate the Girl Child) to achieve this record.

Largest Envelope - In tribute to the Indian Prime Minister's

"Make in India" initiative, Dr. Pillai created a 4000 square meter envelope using waste paper to achieve this record.

Attempted - **70000 Candles on a 210 kg Cake** - To celebrate the 70th Indian Independence Day, Dr. Pillai attempted to light 70,000 candles on a 210 kg cake, which was recorded in World Records India.

Attempted - **Documentary on Dhamek Stupa of Sarnath in 17 Languages** - Dr. Pillai attempted to create a documentary on the Dhamek Stupa of Sarnath, dubbing it in 17 different languages. The result of this attempt is currently awaiting confirmation from the Guinness World Records.

Dr. Pillai is skilled in teaching the Bhagavad Gita, a Hindu scripture, and is popular among young people. He has helped many young people improve their lives through his motivational teachings.

In addition to teaching, he has composed and sung numerous Sanskrit Bhajans and patriotic songs.

He has also written and directed several short films and documentaries for awareness campaigns, and has volunteered with the police in both UP and Kerala to spread awareness about various issues through videos and photography.

Incredibly, he has produced and directed over 100 documentaries about the city of Varanasi, all on his own.

He has also helped and guided more than 25 boys and girls to achieve world records through creative and innovative methods. He is a multifaceted person who uses his intellect and the blessings given to him by God to excel in various areas. He is both a teacher and a student, always learning and teaching, and is able to master any subject he comes across.

He is a selfless social activist and motivational speaker who has overcome struggles and failures to become a successful and enthusiastic individual with a rich life experience.

In addition to his work with the Bhagavad Gita, he is also an efficient Tarot card reader, Astro-Vastu consultant, and a talented singer and composer. He has sung the entire Ram Charita Manas and Bhagavad Gita in his own compositions, and has sung the phrase "Lokah Samastha Sukhino Bhavantu" in 50 different languages. He is currently working on a detailed and scientific study of Vedas, Upanishads, Puranas, and the Bhagavad Gita. He has also composed and sung the Hanuman Chalisa and Gayatri Mantra in 108 and 1008 different compositions, respectively.

Awards - Four Times Guinness World Records, Winner of Mahatma Gandhi Vishwa Shanti Puraskar, Mahatma Gandhi Global Peace Ambassador, Kashi Ratna Award, Dr. APJ Abdul Kalam Motivational Person of the Year 2017, Mother Teresa Award, Indira Gandhi Priyadarshini Award, Bharat Vikas Ratna Award, Udyog Ratna Award, Vigyan Prasar Award, Poorvanchal Ratn Samman.

Preface

The Ramayan of Tulsidas is one of the most revered and celebrated texts in the Hindu tradition. It is a retelling of the ancient epic Ramayana, written by the poet-saint Tulsidas in the 16th century. The Ramcharitmanas, as it is commonly known, is considered a masterpiece of devotional literature and is widely read and studied in India and abroad.

In this book, "The Ramayan of Tulsidas - The Divine Journey of Dharma, an Overview of the Ramcharitmanas", we delve into the rich and profound messages of the Ramcharitmanas. Each chapter provides an overview of the key themes and messages present in the text, with a focus on the overarching message of dharma, or righteousness.

It explores the story of King Dashratha, who is forced to send his beloved son Rama into exile, despite his desire to keep him by his side. This chapter highlights the importance of fulfilling one's duties and responsibilities, even if it means going against one's own wishes.

It also delves into the story of Sita's abduction by the demon king Ravana and Rama's quest to rescue her. This chapter explores the theme of devotion, as Rama's love for Sita is the driving force behind his actions. It also touches upon the themes of sacrifice and the power of love.

The story then focuses on the battle between Rama and Ravana, and the eventual victory of Rama. This chapter explores the themes of good versus evil, and the importance of standing up for what is right and fighting against injustice.

Then it explores the reunion of Rama and Sita and their eventual return to Ayodhya. This chapter highlights the importance of forgiveness and the power of redemption. It also touches on the theme of the triumph of good over evil.

This book provides an overview of the key messages and themes that have been explored throughout the Ramcharitmanas. It highlights the importance of dharma, or righteousness, in one's life and the ultimate victory of good over evil.

This book serves as a comprehensive guide to the Ramcharitmanas, providing an overview of the key themes and messages present in the text. It serves as an invaluable resource for anyone looking to deepen their understanding of this sacred text and the wisdom it imparts.

I

Goswami Tulsidas

Tulsidas began writing the Ramcharitmanas in Ayodhya in Vikram Samvat 1631 (1574 CE) on the ninth day of the month of Chaitra, which is the birthday of Rama, Rama Navami. He composed the epic at Ayodhya, Varanasi, and Chitrakoot, during the reign of Emperor Akbar (1556-1605 CE), making him a contemporary of William Shakespeare.

The Ramcharitmanas is written in the vernacular Awadhi language and is considered by some to be a poetic retelling of the events of the Sanskrit epic Ramayana by Valmiki. However, it is not a word-to-word copy of the Valmiki Ramayana, nor an abridged re-telling of the latter. It contains elements from many other Ramayanas written earlier in Sanskrit and other Indian dialects, as well as stories from Puranas.

According to Tulsidas, he received the story through his guru, Narharidas, and stored it in his mind (Mānasa) for a long time before writing it down. Some understand this passage of the Ramcharitmanas to mean that Tulsidas, as a naïve young boy, initially could not grasp the story fully, and his guru graciously repeated it.

"Rama is the ocean of mercy and kindness,
the embodiment of compassion and love."
- Ramcharitmanas

II

Introduction to Ramcharit Manas

Ramcharitmanas, written by the 16th-century Indian bhakti poet Tulsidas, is an epic poem in the Awadhi language based on the Ramayana. Popularly known as Tulsi Ramayana, Tulsikrit Ramayana, or Tulsidas Ramayana, the word Ramcharitmanas literally translates to 'Lake of the Deeds of Rama'.

It is considered one of the greatest works of Hindu literature and has been acclaimed as the living sum of Indian culture, the tallest tree in the magic garden of medieval Indian poetry, the greatest book of all devotional literature, and the best and most trustworthy guide to the popular living faith of the Indian people.

Tulsidas was a great scholar of Sanskrit, but he wanted the story of Rama to be accessible to the general public, as many Apabhramsa languages had evolved from Sanskrit and few people could understand it. Thus, he chose to write in Awadhi, despite facing criticism from the Sanskrit scholars of Varanasi for being a bhasha (vernacular) poet.

His work was widely accepted and made the story of Rama available to the common man to sing, meditate, and perform on. The writing of Ramcharitmanas also heralded many a cultural tradition, most significantly that of the tradition of Ramlila, the dramatic enactment of the text. It is considered a work belonging to the Saguna school of the Bhakti movement in Hindi literature.

"Rama maintaince patience, forgiving and compassionate even to his enemies."
- Ramcharitmanas

ॐ

III

Lord Shriram and Ayodhya

Lord Shriram, the seventh incarnation of Vishnu, is one of the most important gods in Hinduism. His story and connections to Ayodhya, the ancient city in India, have been the subject of many religious text, sacred art, and devotion throughout the ages.

The story of Lord Shriram's connection to Ayodhya starts with his father, King Dashratha. When Dashratha died, the kingdom was passed to his oldest son Lord Shriram and the other sons. Shriram moved the capital to Ayodhya, where he was beloved by the citizens. He established excellent systems of justice, economics, and fairness that have become part of the local folklore.

The citizens of Ayodhya felt a deep devotion to Shriram. There is a popular belief that Ayodhya was so safe and prosperous under him that there were no thefts, contagious diseases, poverty or distress. He was an ideal king, who inspired everyone around him with his divine qualities. Even those who were not Hindu ascribed to his virtues and ethics, and his past was revered by all.

Ayodhya is also deeply connected to Shriram's wife, Sita. It was here that she was banished to after being branded with infidelity by Shriram, and it was also here, surrounded by her people, that she was vindicated and returned to Shriram's side. This story of tragedy and ultimate joy creates a special bond between the people of Ayodhya and the divine couple, a bond that still exists today.

The devotion the citizens of Ayodhya have towards Lord Shriram is more than just veneration. Legend has it that Ayodhya is the only city in India that Lord Shriram visits every year. Every Diwali, on the day of Lord Vishnu's incarnation, Shriram appears in the city and lights millions of lamps throughout the cityscape. The devotion of the people of Ayodhya is so great that they beleive they can see him in every lamp that is lit.

These connections and devotion to Lord Shriram and Ayodhya is still evident today, both in the city and in Hindu tradition and practice. Every year thousands of devotees visit Ayodhya for special festivals and events to honor Shriram. devotion and reverence for Lord Shriram remains one of the most important elements of Hindu faith and culture.

Quote

"The mind is restless, like a monkey, difficult to control. Without Ram, by whose grace it is stilled, how can one obtain peace?"
- Ramcharitmanas

IV

About Lord Ram's Brothers

When we think about Lord Ram, we often overlook the fact that he had four brothers: Bharata, Lakshmana, Satrughna, and Shatrughana. While Ram was the eldest son of King Dasharatha, each of the four brothers played an important role during his exile and conquest of Lanka.

Bharata was the second eldest son of King Dasharatha and Queen Kaushalya. He was born to Queen Kaikeyi, Dasharatha's second wife after an extraordinary battle. After discovering that his father had made a promise to Kaikeyi, Bharata begged Lord Ram to stay in Ayodhya. When Ram refused, Bharata assumed leadership of the kingdom on Ram's behalf. Under his rule, the kingdom flourished and he fulfilled his responsibilities with dignity and honour. His firmness and patience made him the ideal candidate for governing Ayodhya.

Lakshmana was born younger than Bharata and was the brother so closest to Ram. He was assigned as Ram's guard and protector. He was often regarded as an incarnation of Aditya, the sun god, due to his strong sense of loyalty and dedication to Ram. Lakshmana was an exemplary warrior, who stood by Ram's side during their journey to Lanka and ensured that his brother would return successful from his battle against Ravana.

Satrughna was the youngest brother among all four sons of Dasharatha. He was often compared to Lord Vishnu due to his compassionate and devoted nature. He fought alongside Ram and was successful in killing Lavansa, the King of Mathura and in defeating the demons Ahiravana and Kirmir. He subsequently married the princess of Mathura, and after the war had ended, Satrughna was crowned King of Mathura.

The fourth and youngest brother was Shatrughna. He sided with Bharata, who had appointed him as the commander of his armies. He faced off with the demons with cunning strategies and great courage, leading him to become a skilled warrior in his own right. He was also responsible for establishing the kingdom of Madhu, which had grown wealthy and prosperous under his rule.

Thus, the four brothers of Lord Ram are remembered in Hindu mythology for their admirable qualities, strength, and courage. They each played an important role in the famous Ramayana and had a significant influence on the outcome of the war against Lanka. While Ram is often celebrated as the hero of the story, his four brothers should never be forgotten as they too contributed greatly to his success.

ꕥ

Quote

"Every effort is fruitless that is not backed by forbearance, detachment and heroism."
- Ramcharitmanas

ꙮ

V

Ram's Wife Sita

In Hindu mythology, Lord Rama and his wife Sita are two of the avatars of Vishnu, furthering their typification as a divine pair. Lord Rama is forever known as the model prince, ideal king, and sate of Dharma, while Sita has been idealized as the epitome of wifely and womanly virtues. The tale of this divine pair has been told and mythologised for ages, intertwined within Indian art, literature, and culture.

The story starts in the kingdom of Ayodhya, where Rama was born to King Dasharatha and Queen Kausalya of the Ikshvaku line. Determined to adhere to Dharma, the king promised his eldest son Bharta the throne only for him to go back on his word and declare Rama as the new king. This resulted in the then-crown-prince variously known as Sita, venturing into exile with his brother Lakshman and loving wife Sita, for 14 years.

Sharing a deep and unwavering love with one another, Rama and Sita persevered through every trial and tribulation. Throughout their exile, they adhered to the path of righteousness, not once faltering in their honour or commitment to each other. Soon enough, through the help of Hanuman and the monkeys of Kishkindha, their exile came to a sudden end.

Returning to Ayodhya, Rama and Sita were welcomed with open-arms and were finally crowned as the rightful king and queen. For the next few years, the two served shoulder-to-shoulder with Rama upholding Dharma and Sita keeping her husband's wishes ever close.

However, even a story as beautiful as this was not exempt from a possible twist of tragedy. After hearing various rumours of Sita's supposed unfaithfulness, Rama as per his sense of Dharma, asked his beloved wife Sita to prove her innocence. After taking a stringent test of fire, Sita emerged unscathed, cements her purity of mind and body.

Even so, Rama felt the need for Sita to further prove her innocence and thus dismissed her from his kingdom and sent her into the forest. Dejected, Sita expressed her wishes to forever stay in the bowels of nature, to live a life of solace and purity.

By this act, Rama paid tribute to his sense of Dharma, adhering to the system he had championed in his life. Despite his resolve, Rama's love and respect for his wife did not waver, never truly leaving her behind, instead, sending his devotee Hanuman to perpetually shadow her through her adventures. Surrendering to her fate, Sita emerged as a character in her own right, signifying strength and a sense of duty.

The story was eventually concluded by Rama's coronation and Sita.

Quote

"The path of devotion is the easiest; it is like a child's play."
- Ramcharitmanas

ꕥ

VI

Ravan of Lanka

Ravana is one of the most significant villains in Hindu mythology. He is the primary antagonist in the epic poem Ramayana, which chronicles the tale of Rama, the seventh avatar of Vishnu. In the epic, Ravana kidnaps Rama's beloved wife Sita and holds her captive on the island of Lanka. In the ensuing war, Rama defeats Ravana and rescues Sita from captivity.

Ravana is said to have been born around 5,000 years ago to a great sage called Vishrava and a demoness by the name of Kaikeshi. Ravana was an expert in the Vedas and the Upanishads, as well as a master of many languages and an accomplished scholar of Sankya and yoga. He was an expert in warfare and a great devotee of Shiva.

Ravana had a remarkable ability to fly and could travel through the air with his chariot. He also had several magical powers at his disposal and was able to control the elements of nature. He was said to possess ten heads and twenty arms and was powerful enough to challenge even the gods.

Ravana had several brothers and sisters, the most significant of whom were Kubera and Kumbhakarna. He was also the father of a powerful yet humble son, Akshaya Kumar, and a beautiful daughter, Mandodari. He had several wives, but the most prominent and loyal was Mandodari. Ravana had grand ambitions and was very knowledgeable about politics and diplomacy. He was a ruler who was feared and respected by other leaders in the region.

Ravana is often portrayed as a villain in popular culture, but through his story, we can unearth many values. He showed great resilience and strength, as well as a steadfast commitment to his family and allies. He also demonstrated loyalty and compassion to those who were loyal to him.

Ravana's story in the Ramayana has become a symbol of morality and righteousness through the ages. His story is an example of how evil can be defeated and virtue can prevail. The story of Ravana presents us with lessons on how delusions can be overcome and how truth and justice can eventually triumph.

Quote

"He who chants Rama's name even once, obtains the merit of performing many Yajnas."
- Ramcharitmanas

ꕥ

VII

Lord Hanuman

Lord Hanuman is one of the most beloved characters in the Hindu epic, the Ramayana. His feats of strength and courage throughout the story have made him a beloved figure in Hinduism and a symbol of loyalty, devotion and unshakable faith. Though he is not a major protagonist in the epic, his influence on the story and its characters has been profound.

Hanuman was born to a divine wind god and an apsara, resulting in him being an exceptional being with superhuman strength and extraordinary powers. His strength and other capabilities are evidenced in the Ramayana by his ability to battle Ravana's huge army of demons and his flying across the ocean to Lanka in search of Rama's abducted wife Sita.

Hanuman is the hero who guides Rama and Lakshman throughout their 14-year exile, ultimately helping them to vanquish Ravana and his armies, thereby restoring Rama to his rightful place as king. He does this by protecting their kingdom from the demons, helping them to meet allies in their quest and rescuing Sita from captivity.

When in trouble, Hanuman is Rama's greatest defender. He risks his life to protect Rama and his wife in battle, often demonstrating god-like strength and power. As an example, when Angada, Ravana's son, challenges Hanuman's strength, the godly monkey effortlessly lifts an entire mountain and carries it over to the enemy, demonstrating his sheer strength and relentlessness.

Lord Hanuman is also known for his strong commitment to dharma and spiritual purity. He is an obedient devotee of Lord Rama and vows to follow him without fail, no matter the cost. Throughout the epic, we also see Hanuman's devotion and humility. His relationships with other characters offer profound lessons in morality and friendship.

Lord Hanuman's willingness to go above and beyond to serve Rama's cause without any personal gain has made him an enduring symbol of loyalty, faithfulness, and piety. He serves as a moral compass for his fellow characters and an example to us of how to be a selfless and devoted individual.

In the end, Hanuman's actions and commitment demonstrate his unbridled devotion and loyalty to Rama, his determination and strength, and his unparalleled courage. He has become an integral part of the Ramayana, and his character will continue to be admired by generations to come.

Quote

"The more one speaks of Rama's glory, the more one is blessed with peace."
- Ramcharitmanas

Chapterwise Overview

Balkand

Ayodyhakand

Kishkindakand

Aranyakand

Sunderkand

Lanka Kand

Uttara Kand

VIII

Balkand

Tulsidas begins the story of Ramcharitmanas with an invocation to various deities, his guru, and saints who have come before him and those who will come after him. He pays homage to Valmiki for bringing the Ramayana to the devotees of Rama. He then introduces and praises the characters of the epic, beginning with the holy city of Ayodhya, the birthplace of Rama, and Dasharatha, the king of Ayodhya and Rama's father, as well as his queens Kausalya, Kaikeyi, and Sumitra. Tulsidas also praises King Janaka (the father-in-law of Rama) and his family, and the brothers of Rama - Bharata, Lakshman, and Shatrughna. He also sings the praises of Hanuman, the constant companion of Rama, Sugriva, the monkey king, and Jambavan, the leader of bears. Finally, the characters of Sita and Rama are introduced.

The story of Ramcharitmanas then begins with the meeting of two sages - Bharadwaj and Yajnavalkya. Bharadwaj asks Yajnavalkya to narrate in detail the story of Rama. Yajnavalkya begins by explaining how Shiva told the story of Rama to his wife Parvati, including the story of Sati's self-immolation, the destruction of her father Daksha's sacrifice, the rebirth of Sati as Parvati, and her marriage to Shiva. Shiva then explains five different reasons why Rama incarnated on earth in different ages (Kalpa). Each of these stories is discussed in detail, with the primary message being that Rama incarnated on earth to protect the righteous who follow the path of Dharma. The story then moves to the birth of Ravana and his brothers. After this point, the narration is done at different times.

The story now moves to the abode of Brahma, where Brahma and the other Hindu Devas were gathered, trying to find a way to rid the earth of Ravana and his evil deeds. Unable to come up with a solution, they prayed to Shiva for guidance. Shiva told them that they did not need to look far for the Supreme God, as He resides in the hearts of His devotees. All the Devas then prayed to the Supreme Brahman/Vishnu to save them from the demons. Brahman, filled with compassion, announced in an Akashvani that He would be born in the Sun Dynasty to save the Devas and His devotees from the demons. The story then moves to Ayodhya, where King Dasharatha realizes he is getting old and still has no sons. He expresses his distress to Sage Vasistha, the family guru, and seeks a way forward. Vasistha comforts Dasharatha and tells him he will have four sons. He then requests Rishyasringa to perform the Putrakām yajna (vedic yajna for the birth of sons). On the ninth day of the Chaitra month, during the shukla period, Rama and his brothers were born. The story then moves on and Rama and his brothers are now grown-up boys. Sage Vishvamitra arrives at Dasharatha's royal court, where the King receives him with great honor. Vishvamitra had been living in the forest and performing great sacrifices, but the demons Maricha and Subahu kept desecrating the ceremonial offerings. Knowing that Rama had been born to protect his devotees, Vishvamitra asked the King for a favor: to let his sons accompany him to the forest."

Reluctantly, the King agreed. Rama had already known why Vishvamitra had asked him to come along. He promised the sage that he would obey his orders. Lakshman then killed Subahu and Rama killed Tataka and defeated Maricha, the terrifying demons.

Vishvamitra watched as Rama broke the bow to win Sita's hand in marriage. The story then shifted to the rescue of Ahalya. Rama, Lakshman, and Vishvamitra went on a journey and arrived at the beautiful kingdom of the Videhas, Mithila. The King of Mithila, Janaka, welcomed the great sage and asked who the two boys accompanying him were. Janaka was overwhelmed with emotion as he could sense the true purpose of their mission. The brothers then explored the beautiful city and visited Janaka's garden. This part of the manās is significant as it shows the first meeting of Rama and Sita.

King Janaka arranged a Swayamvara ceremony for his daughter Sita, a Vedic ritual in which a prospective bride selects her groom from among a group of suitors. When Sita saw Rama in Janaka's garden, she fell in love with him at first sight and prayed to Parvati that she would get Rama as her husband. Janaka sent a messenger to invite Rama, Laksman, and Sage Vishvamitra to the ceremony. He set a condition to identify the right groom for Sita: the great bow of Shiva, Pinaka, was placed in the arena and any suitor who could string it would marry Sita. Many princes tried but failed to even move the bow, causing Janaka to worry if the earth had become devoid of brave men. Lakshman was angered by this statement and retorted that no one should talk like this when the Sun Dynasty was present.

Rama calmed him and Vishwamitra asked him to break the bow and make Janaka happy. Rama stepped in and effortlessly lifted and strung the bow, then broke it with a swift move. This caused a loud noise that disturbed the great sage Parashurama in his meditation and he stormed into the arena, vowing to kill whoever had dared to break the bow of Lord Shiva. Lakshman argued with Parashurama, showing little respect for the sage who was known for his bursts of anger and slaying those who opposed him. Eventually, Rama brought him around and Parashurama realized Rama's true nature as the ultimate Brahman, paid his respects, and left for the forests for meditation. Sita placed the wreath of victory around Rama's neck in accordance with the rules of the Swayamvara, and they were wed.

King Janaka was deeply devoted to his daughter Sita, so he wanted to give her the grandest wedding possible. He sent messengers to Ayodhya to inform Dasharatha and his family about the marriage of Rama and Sita and invited them to the ceremony. Dasharatha and his entourage, including Shiva, Brahma, and the Devas in human form, set off for Mithila. Not only were Rama and Sita married, but Bharat and Mandavi, Lakshman and Urmila, and Shatrughna and Shrutakirti were also wed.

The wedding was a magnificent affair, the likes of which

had never been seen before. After the festivities, Rama and Sita returned to Ayodhya, where there was a huge celebration and much joy.

MESSAGE

The First chapter of the Ramcharitmanas, titled 'Ayodhya Kand', is an invocation to Lord Rama and the beginning of the epic. It is believed that the recitation of Ramcharitmanas brings divine grace and peace to the household. The chapter is an ode to Lord Rama and is a prayer to seek his mercy and grace. The chapter begins with a description of the greatness of Lord Rama and his divine form. It speaks of Rama's many virtues and his magnanimity. It also describes the various qualities of Rama's devotees and how they are blessed with fortune and good health.

The chapter also speaks of how Rama is the embodiment of truth, compassion and justice and how he is the protector of the weak and the helpless. The chapter also speaks of how Rama is the embodiment of knowledge and the ultimate source of wisdom and knowledge. The chapter also speaks of how Lord Rama is the destroyer of evils and the one who dispels darkness from the world. It also speaks of how Rama is the one who can grant salvation to his devotees and also how he can grant protection to those who seek it. The chapter also speaks of how reciting Ramcharitmanas can bring peace and prosperity to a household. It also speaks of how reciting

Ramcharitmanas can bring blessings to one's life and can provide protection and guidance to the devotee. Overall, the first chapter of the Ramcharitmanas speaks of the greatness of Lord Rama and his divine form.

Quote

"Rama is a constant reminder of the power of truth, courage and virtue."
- Ramcharitmanas

ꕤ

IX

Ayodhyakand

Ayodhya was known as a heavenly place ever since Rama and Sita returned from Mithila. As King Dasharatha was getting older, he wanted to make Rama the Prince Regent. He planned to start the coronation ceremonies the next day. However, the Devas were worried that Rama would stay in Ayodhya and not go after the wicked Ravana. They asked Goddess Saraswati for help.

King Dasharatha had three wives. Queen Kaushalya was the main queen and the mother of Rama. Queen Kaikeyi was the mother of Bharata and Queen Sumitra was the mother of Lakshman and Shatrughna. Saraswati decided to influence the mind of one of Queen Kaikeyi's maidservants, Manthara. Manthara had evil intentions and she spoke to Queen Kaikeyi in a rude and arrogant way. She criticized Kaikeyi for supporting the King's plan to make Rama the Prince Regent, when she thought Bharata would be a better king. At that time, Bharata was visiting his uncle in Kaikeya country and was unaware of what was happening in Ayodhya. Manthara reminded Queen Kaikeyi of the two boons that the King had promised her. Kaikeyi went to the royal palace, where the King was giving audience to his queens. Dasharatha was shocked and worried when he saw Kaikeyi in the sulking chamber, while the people of Ayodhya were excited and looking forward to Rama's coronation.

Queen Kaikeyi shocked King Dasharatha when she spoke harshly to him and reminded him of the two boons he had promised her. She asked him to make her son, Bharata, the Prince Regent and to send Rama away to the forest for 14 years. Despite Dasharatha's pleas, Queen Kaikeyi was unmoved. Eventually, the king was so overwhelmed with emotion that he broke down. His assistant, Sumantra, sent for Rama and asked him to meet his father.

Queen Kaikeyi explained to Rama why she had asked for the boons. Although Rama was actually the Supreme Personality of Godhead incarnated on earth, he accepted his stepmother's request as it served his purpose. The people of Ayodhya were angry with Queen Kaikeyi, but she was sure she was doing the right thing. Rama tried to convince Lakshman and Sita not to join him, but they refused. The scene became very emotional as Rama, Sita, and Lakshman said goodbye to their mothers before going to Dasharatha to take their leave. Despite his attempts to talk Sita out of it, Dasharatha was unsuccessful.

The residents of Ayodhya could not bear the thought of being away from Rama and decided to join him in the forest. So, in the dead of the night, Rama, Sita, Lakshman, and Sumantra left the city and ventured into the forest. They eventually arrived at Sringaverapur, where they met

Guha, the Nishad king. After that, they reached Prayag, the holy city where the Rivers Ganges, Yamuna, and Saraswati meet. There, Rama was warmly welcomed by the people living on the banks of the Yamuna. He then went to Chitrakoot dham, where he met Sage Valmiki, the author of the Ramayan. Valmiki was amazed by Rama's true opulence and sang his praises. Tulsidas also took the opportunity to describe the beauty of Chitrakoot with some inspiring poetry.

Rama asked Sumantra to return to Ayodhya, which made him very sad. He not only wanted to stay with Rama, but he was also afraid of going back and facing the anger of the citizens of Ayodhya. However, Rama managed to persuade him to go back. When Sumantra returned to Ayodhya, he met Dasharatha, who asked him about Rama's whereabouts. The pain of separation from Rama was too much for Dasharatha, and he passed away while crying out Rama's name.

Sage Vashishtha was aware that Rama would not be coming back to the kingdom, so he quickly sent an envoy to summon Bharata and Shatrughna to Ayodhya. When Bharata heard what had happened, he was filled with anger and regret, blaming himself for Rama's departure. He also harshly criticized his mother, Queen Kaikeyi. Shatrughna then encountered Manthara and, in a fit of rage, beat her. When they reached Queen Kaushalya, they saw her in a state of distress. Bharata begged for her forgiveness and wept loudly, while the Queen tried to comfort him. She asked him to fulfill his duty and rule Ayodhya, but Bharata could not bear the thought of sitting on the throne without his father and brothers. The funeral of King Dasharatha was held, and Bharata and Shatrughna decided to go to the forest and ask Rama to come back to Ayodhya and take the throne. Many citizens, as well as the royal family, who had been grieving since Rama left, decided to join the brothers on their journey.

The Nishads saw the approaching royal party and became suspicious. Guha approached Bharata to understand his motive for bringing such a large group to the forest. He suspected that Bharata had some hidden agenda. However, Bharata showed his deep love for Rama, which moved Guha to tears. The royal procession then continued on to Chitrakoot. Lakshman noticed the huge army of people with Bharata and immediately began to scold him. Rama countered this by praising Bharata's greatness, leaving Lakshman feeling remorseful for his harsh words. Eventually, Bharata arrived at Chitrakoot, where the brothers were reunited. They all mourned the passing of their father and performed his Shraddha (obsequies) with Sage Vashistha leading the ceremony.

Despite Bharata's best efforts, Rama remained true to his word and vowed to fulfill Kaikeyi's wish. Bharata said he could not sit on the throne while Rama was in the forest. He asked Rama for his sandals, which he would place on the throne and act as Rama's representative, not as a full-fledged king.

With much sadness and pain, Bharata left Rama and returned to Ayodhya. He refused to live in the kingdom while Rama was in exile and instead lived like a hermit in a nearby town called Nandigram.

MESSAGE

The Ramayana is a timeless epic that is full of positive teachings and messages. Ayodhya Kand, in particular, talks of the importance of dharma - or righteousness - that speaks to us even today. This episode tells us how the right course of action can bring happiness even if it requires great sacrifice. Lord Rama's unwavering devotion to dharma and justice teach us the power of restraint and patience in difficult times as well as universal brotherhood. The qualities inherent in leaders such as truthfulness and honesty are glorified here which helps to develop good character, something so essential for peace and harmony.

"Rama is the embodiment of Dharma, the symbol of righteousness and justice."
- Ramcharitmanas

ೞ

X

Aranyakand

Rama, Sita and Lakshman wandered through the forest and eventually came across the hermitage of Sage Atri. Atri was overjoyed to see them and his wife, Anasuya, warmly embraced Sita. Anasuya then spoke to Sita at length about the duties of a devoted wife.

The trio continued their journey and encountered Viradha, who attempted to capture Sita. Rama, however, killed him by burying him in a ditch. They then visited the ashram of Sage Sarabhanga, who advised them to seek shelter with Sage Sutiksna. As Rama approached Sutiksna, the latter emerged from his meditation and told Rama that he had been expecting him and had even refused the offer of entering the heavenly planets.

Thirteen years passed and the group eventually met with Sage Agastya. Rama paid his respects to the sage, who gifted him divine weapons and advised him to venture further into the forest and into the region of Dandaka. There, they met with the eagle, Jatayu. Following Agastya's advice,

Rama, Sita and Lakshman took up abode at Panchavati and built a beautiful ashram. Lakshman became nostalgic of the past and began to speak harshly about Kaikeyi. Rama, however, calmed him down and reminded him that it was wrong to speak of his mother in such a way.

The story takes an unexpected turn when Rama, Sita, and Lakshman are approached by Surpanakha, the sister of the demon-king Ravana. She is instantly taken with Rama and tries to win his affections. Rama kindly explains that he is already married and suggests that she should try to win the affections of Lakshman, who is unmarried. However, Lakshman also rejects her advances. Feeling insulted, Surpanakha attempts to hurt Sita, but Lakshman quickly draws his sword and cuts off her ear lobes and nose. Humiliated, Surpanakha leaves the forest and goes to her brothers Khara and Dusana. Furious at the treatment of their sister, they set out to kill Rama. But, Rama is victorious and defeats both of them.

Surpanakha is filled with rage and visits Ravana in Lanka. She tells him what happened and Ravana calls upon his old friend Maricha. Ravana devises a plan and orders Maricha to disguise himself as a golden deer so that he can kidnap Sita. Maricha is scared, knowing that Rama is powerful, but he realizes that he will die either way since Ravana will kill him if he refuses. Ravana and Maricha then leave for Rama's forest home.

Maricha took his position and instantly Sita was attracted to his deer form. Rama knew of Ravana's intentions and ordered Sita to place her shadow (Maya Sita) in her place, while she would hide in the fire. She asked Rama time and time again to hunt for the deer and bring it to her. Rama ran after the deer and soon found himself quite a far distance away from the ashram. He released an arrow and hit the deer. Impersonating Rama's voice, Marich shouted out to Lakshman to help him. Sita heard the cry and ordered Lakshman to go help his brother. Ravana, posing as a begging minstrel, used this opportunity to forcibly kidnap Sita from the ashram.

Jatayu, the eagle, saw Ravana's sinful act and attempted to fight him, but Ravana had too much power and cut off Jatayu's wings, leaving him for dead. Rama and Lakshman returned to find the ashram empty and anxiously set out to find Sita. They soon found the severely wounded eagle, who died in Rama's lap and received liberation.

As they continued to search for Sita, they came across the hermitage of Shabari. Tulsidas says that Shabari washed the feet of Rama with tears from her eyes and fed him half-eaten wild berries to ensure he only got sweet ones. She was given liberation by Rama. The brothers then headed towards the Pampasarovar lake.

MESSAGE

The Aranyakanda of the Ramayana is a tale of significant spiritual teachings, offering a profound and powerful message on how to live a meaningful life full of selflessness and courage. The story revolves around Lord Rama's journey away from his beloved kingdom in search for his wife Sita who was kidnapped by the demon king

Ravana. During his arduous voyage, Rama takes part in numerous battles against evil forces but remains grounded in humility and morality the entire time. Through this story, we learn valuable lessons about developing wisdom, courage, and resilience even when facing insurmountable obstacles. We also gain an insight into the nature of niyatam (the principle of one's intention), recognizing that all our actions should be underpinned by mindful service to others and not through selfish desire or greed. These timeless teachings offer us both guidance and perspective today in leading us towards living with peace, nobility, and purpose.

"Serve those devotedly who serve you"

ꙮ

XI

Kishkindakand

In the Rishyamukha mountains, Sugriva spots Rama and Laksman at the base of the hills. He asks Hanuman if he believes they have been sent by his brother Bali. Hanuman, pretending to be a Brahmin, meets the brothers and recognizes Rama as a divine incarnation. He surrenders to Rama and informs him that his king, Sugriva, wishes to be friends with them and will help them find Sita. Rama enquires why Sugriva resides in the mountains instead of Kishkindha and learns of his feud with Bali. Rama expresses empathy and decides to aid Sugriva in his search for Sita in exchange for his help. Rama kills Bali and installs Sugriva as king of Kishkindha, and Bali's son Angada as prince regent.

However, Sugriva becomes too absorbed in his new royal lifestyle and forgets his agreement with Rama, making Rama very angry. Rama orders Lakshman to bring Sugriva to him. Lakshman enters the court and threatens to burn the city, causing Sugriva to ask Hanuman to intervene. Lakshman then brings Sugriva to Rama, and upon seeing him, Sugriva apologizes and begs for forgiveness.

Sugriva immediately commands the gathering of the region's bear and monkey communities. Armies of bears and monkeys are sent out in all directions to search for Sita. Rama knows that only Hanuman has the capability to find Sita, and asks him to narrate the anguish of separation from her, before giving him his ring. Hanuman is joined by Angad, Nala, Nila, Kesari and Jambavan, as well as many others, as they head south. When the army approaches the coast, Jambavan and Angad spot a cave by the ocean's shore.

The cave is occupied by Sampati, who is actually Jatayu's older brother. In the conversation that ensues, Angad explains that Jatayu died while serving Rama and thereafter Sampati narrates his biography. He tells the monkeys that he is certain that Sita is held captive in Ashok Vatika in Lanka. The island is 400 miles away, and requires someone who can jump the distance. Jambavan deduces that Hanuman is the only one capable of such a feat.

MESSAGE

The Essence and message of the Kishkindakanda of the Ramayana is one of a moral lesson. It serves to illustrate the impact of our actions, to inspire us to love selflessly in all matters, and to ensure that only truth will prevail in the end. The cause and effect relationship behind our deeds is highlighted through characters such as Sugriva, Hanuman, Rama and Sita who were put into difficult or

compromising situations due to their words or actions, yet ultimately pull through because their faith in dharma remains steadfast no matter what may come. Ultimately, it teaches us that it is best always to stay true to ourselves and never compromise on our values--a core message from this ancient epic that still resonates with readers today.

"Where there is attachment, worry follows"

ꟷ

XII
Sunderkand

Hanuman tells Sita that he is hungry and asks for her permission to eat fruits from the grove. He not only eats, but also manages to destroy large parts of it. He easily kills one of Ravana's sons, Prince Akshaya. Indrajit arrives in the grove and Hanuman allows himself to be captured. He is brought in front of the king of Lanka, Ravana. Ravana orders his death, but Vibhishan reminds him that Hanuman is an envoy and cannot be killed according to religious principles. Ravana decides to humiliate Hanuman by setting his tail on fire. Large amounts of cloth are tied to his tail and soaked in oil. Hanuman chants the name of Rama and his tail begins to grow longer and more cloth and oil is used. He changes from his small form into a gigantic form and decides to set alight the whole of Lanka.

He returns to the ocean to extinguish his tail and then goes to Sita to reassure her that the next time she sees him, it will be with Rama. He bids farewell to Sita and leaps back towards Angad and Jambavan. The monkey army then ventures back to where Sugriva, Rama and Lakshman are waiting. On arrival, Hanuman explains all that happened and immediately an army is prepared to go south towards Lanka.

Meanwhile, in Lanka, both Mandodari and Vibhishan ask Ravana to return Sita to Rama. Ravana takes great offense to this suggestion and begins to insult Vibhishan particularly. He tells him he has no need for a weakling like him and that he is no longer needed. Vibhishan decides to join Rama at Kishkindha. Vibhishan falls at Rama's feet and asks him for protection.

The military carefully considered how to cross the ocean to Lanka. The god of the sea informed Rama of the blessing bestowed upon the monkey brothers, Nila and Nala, granting them the ability to construct a bridge connecting the shore to Lanka.

MESSAGE

Sunderkand is a beautiful section of the Valmiki Ramayana and contains some wonderful messages and teachings that one can benefit from. It works as an inspiring guide to help us get through life's challenges. The main positive message of Sunderkand is that in difficult times, when all hope seems lost, faith and devotion to God will always lead to success. Throughout Sunderkand we are reminded that with determination and focus on our spiritual path, we can overcome the harshest obstacles. We are also encouraged to be truthful, honest, forgiving and tolerant of others - traits which lead

to greater peace and harmony in our lives. Finally, Sunderkand teaches us the importance of a strong sense of right and wrong within ourselves; it encourages us towards lofty aims such as self-improvement and liberation from karma!

"Let not your mind be attached to anything but the Lord"

ꕥ

XIII

Lanka Kand

Jambavan asks Nala and Nila to start constructing a bridge across the sea. The Mānas states that entire mountain ranges were used by Nala and Nila to complete the bridge. Rama remembers Lord Shiva and decides to establish a shrine for Rameswaram. Once the bridge is completed, Rama's army crosses and sets up camp on Mount Suvela. Upon hearing of Rama's army's advancement, Ravana becomes agitated. Mandodari urges Ravana to return Sita to Rama, fearing for his life. Ravana dismisses Rama's power and comforts his wife. His son Prahasta also tries to reinforce Mandodari's sentiment, but to no avail.

Rama sends a warning shot from his camp on Suvela, striking Ravana's crown and royal umbrella. Mandodari once again tries to convince Ravana to return Sita to Rama. Rama asks Jambavan for advice and he suggests sending Angada as a messenger to give Ravana a chance to return Sita. Upon arriving at Ravana's court, Angada, representing Rama, tells Ravana that he still has time to avoid destruction. Ravana insults Angada and his refusal to comply leads to war.

The battle starts fiercely, with Ravana losing half of his army on the first day. Indrajit, Ravana's son, is forced to enter the battle earlier than expected and severely wounds Lakshman with his special weapon, the Saang. Hanuman is ordered to fetch the doctor of Lanka, Sushena, who tells Rama that there is a herb called Sanjivani that can only be found in the Himalayan mountains and is the only hope to save Lakshman. Hanuman reassures Rama that he will find the herb. As Hanuman leaves, Ravana sends the demon Kalanemi to stop him, but Hanuman kills him easily. Hanuman reaches the mountain and can't find the herb, so in frustration, he decides to take the entire mountain to Lanka.

On the way back to Lanka, Hanuman is shot by an arrow by Bharat, who mistakes him for a demon. Hanuman falls to the ground with the mountain. He regains consciousness and recognizes Bharat as Rama's brother. Hanuman delivers the Sanjivani herb to Sushena, who treats Lakshman. Rama embraces Hanuman with great pride and affection. The news of Lakshman's recovery upsets Ravana, who decides to awaken his brother Kumbhakarna. Kumbhakarna kills indiscriminately and causes much destruction. Rama kills him with an arrow.

The death of his brother scares Ravana greatly and his son Indrajit quickly tries to gain more power but is interrupted by Hanuman and Angada. Lakshman fights and kills Indrajit. Rama throws numerous arrows at Ravana but cannot kill him, so he asks Vibhishan for advice and finally kills Ravana. The war ends.

Ravana's funeral takes place and Vibhishan is crowned king of Lanka. Hanuman brings the good news to Sita in Ashok Vatika and Rama and Sita are finally reunited. Rama and the army prepare to leave Lanka and return to Ayodhya. Rama, Sita, Lakshman, and the senior monkeys return in Ravana's flying vehicle, Pushpak Vimaan.

MESSAGE

The epic poem Ramcharitmanas by Tulsidas is full of lessons about life, but perhaps one of the best words of wisdom comes from Lanka Kand. This part of the text talks about how, despite suffering defeat and hardship, we all can rise above our adversities and prevail in the end. It teaches us to never give up hope and stay focused on achieving our goals in life no matter what obstacles might come our way. We should take strength from within ourselves and push forward to build a better future. Lanka Kand reminds us that it's only when we strive to seize victory against all odds that real achievement can be achieved, instilling in us a positive mindset allowing us to reach both worldly gains and inner enlightenment.

"Abandon pride and ego; abandon greed for worldly possessions"

XIV

Uttara Kand

The day before Rama is set to return to Ayodhya after serving his exile, Bharata is worried that Rama hasn't arrived yet. Hanuman meets Bharata and tells him that Rama, Sita and Laksman are on their way. Bharata rushes to Ayodhya to tell the citizens the good news. When Rama's flying chariot, the Pushpak Vimaan, lands in Ayodhya, the citizens chant "Glory be to Ramchandra". Rama, Sita and Laksman greet everyone in the assembly and Rama especially greets Bharata with great affection. Rama is then crowned king of Ayodhya and Lord Shiva arrives to celebrate the event. Rama has twin sons named Lava and Kusha and his other brothers also have two sons each. Sages like Nārad and Sanaka visit Ayodhya to meet Rama and see his great city. The story ends with a description of the current age of Kali Yuga.

MESSAGE

The epic Ramayana is full of positive messages and lessons for us to learn from. In the Uttara Kand, Rama establishes Ramarajya (the reign of Rama), which signifies a period of perfect justice and selfless service. In essence, it gives us a powerful message about what an ideal society should look like - one where harmony, justice, compassion and mutual respect are at its core foundations. It also encourages us to be persistent in our actions and not give up even when things may seem tough or trying - something that we can all apply to our own lives today.

"Whatever comes your way - accept it with faith"

Other Books Of The Author

1. The Moments When I Met God
2. Kashiyile Theertha Pathangal
3. GURU GYAN VANI
4. Abhiprerak Gita
5. ASSI SE JAIN GHAT TAK
6. Hopelessness of Arjuna
7. The Soul and It's True Nature
8. Sense of Action (Karma)
9. Action through Wisdom
10. Action through Wisdom
11. THEORY AND PRACTICAL OF EVERY ACTION
12. LOGICAL UNDERSTANDING OF THE SUPREME
13. THE IMPERISHABLE SUPREME
14. Yatra Nishadraj se Hanuman Ghat Tak
15. Yatra Karnatak Ghat se Raja Ghat Tak
16. Yatra Pandey Ghat se Prayagraj Ghat Tak
17. Yatra Ranjendra Prasad Ghat se Dattatreya Ghat Tak
18. YaatraSindhiya Ghat se Gwaliar Ghat Tak
19. Yatra Mangala Gauri Ghat se Hanuman Gadhi Ghat Tak
20. Yatra Gaay Ghat Se Nishad Ghat Tak
21. MΛΛ GANGA, GIIATEN EVM UTSAV
22. Ganga Arti Dev Deepavali evam Any Utsav
23. Potentials of Digitalized India
24. VEDIC CONSCIOUSNESS
25. A Brief Introduction to Vedic Science
26. Kashi ke Barah Jyotirling
27. IMPACT OF MOTIVATION
28. Let's have a Milky Way Journey
29. Color Therapy in a Nutshell

30. Rigveda in a Nutshell
31. Yajurveda in a Nutshell
32. Samveda in a Nutshell
33. Atharva Veda in a Nutshell
34. Ayushman Bhava - Ayurveda
35. Srimad Bhagavad Gita and Upanishad Connection
36. Srimad Bhagavad Gita - an attempt to summarize each chapter.
37. Facts and Impact of Nakshatra
38. Astro Gems - NAVARATNA
39. Ekadashi - A Concise Overview
40. A Concise View of Hanuman Chalisa
41. Inspirational Gita
42. Nakshatraranyam
43. Summary of 18 Mahapuranas
44. Synopsis of 18 Upa Puranas
45. Rigvediya Upanishads
46. Shukla Yajurvediya Upanishads
47. Krishna Yajurvediya Upanishads
48. Samavediya Upanishads
49. Atharvavediya Upanishads
50. The Seven Great Sages
51. From Rocket Scientist to President Dr. APJ Abdul Kalam
52. The Visionary's Voice - Quotes of Dr. APJ Abdul Kalam
53. The Wisdom of Swami Vivekananda: Insights and Inspiration from a Legendary Spiritual Teacher
54. Ayurvedic Remedies from the Garden
55. Sages and Seers
56. Rising Strong – Motivational Stories of Women
57. Beyond Flames -Mystery stories of Funeral Ghat Manikarnika
58. The Origins of Tulsi: A Look at the Mythological Roots of the Plant"

59. The Holistic Cow: A Look at the Physical, Spiritual, and Cultural Importance of Cows in India
60. Arts of Healing
61. Exploring the Divine
62. Understanding Five Elements
63. The Etymology of Ram
64. Symbols of India
65. Voice of Change (About Speeches of Great Men)
66. She Speaks (About Speeches of Great Women)
67. Patriotism on Celluloid – Brief About Patriotic Films
68. The Music of Motivation: A Brief Guide to Inspirational Film Songs
69. Unlocking the Secrets of the Dashopanishads
70. A Cultural Mosaic
71. Ancient Traditions, Modern Minds
72. Ecos of Ancient Wisdom
73. Beneath the Surface
74. From Temples to Ashrams
75. Sages of the Subcontinent
76. The Art of Healling (Ayurveda, Yoga & Naturopathy)
77. Indian Kitchen
78. The Festivals of India
79. The Indian Epics Retold
80. The Power of Mantras
81. The Indian River Ganges
82. The Indian Architecture
83. Rites of Passage
84. The Indian Silk Road
85. The Indian Literature
86. The Indian Villages
87. The Indian Folks & Crafts
88. The Way of Buddha
89. The Ramayan of Tulsidas

ൠ

Contact

DR. JAGADEESH PILLAI

PhD in Vedic Science

Four Times Guinness World Record Holder

Winner of Mahatma Gandhi Vishwa Shanti Puraskar and Global Peace Ambassador

Gemology, Astro & Vastu Consultant - Spiritual Counselor

Consultant for designing World Record Ideas

Efficient Tarot Card Reader

9839093003

myrichindia@gmail.com

drjagadeeshpillai@facebook

drjagadeeshpillai@instagram

jagadeeshpillai@youtube

www. JAGADEESHPILLAI.com

|| LOKAHA SAMASTHAHA SUKHINO BHAVANTU ||

Printed by Libri Plureos GmbH in Hamburg,
Germany